The Andalusian Knitting
and Netting Book

Eléonore Riego de la Branchardière

Alpha Editions

This Edition Published in 2021

ISBN: 9789355346841

Design and Setting By
Alpha Editions
www.alphaedis.com
Email – info@alphaedis.com

TABLE OF CONTENTS

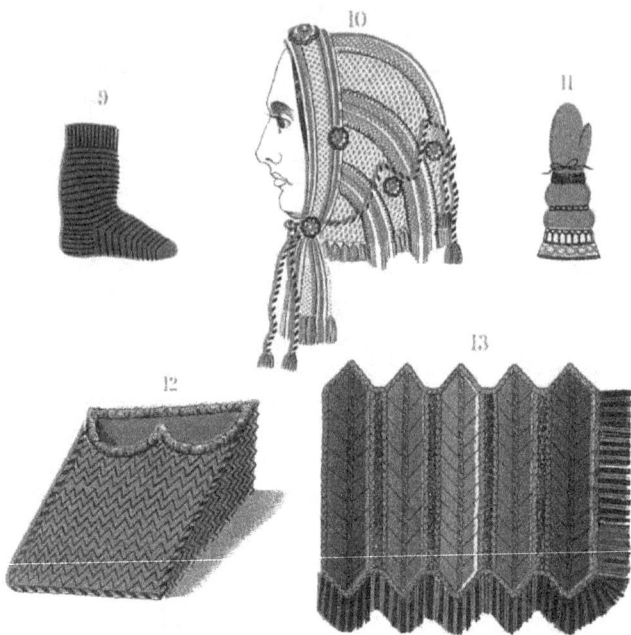

A. Goater, late Taylor & Goater, Nottingham.

THE WAISTBAND

Commence with Magenta wool and pins No. 14, the wool is to be used doubled throughout the waistband. Cast on 34 stitches.

1st row—Knit 2 together, knit the rest plain.

2nd row—Slip the 1st stitch, knit the rest plain.

Repeat these 2 rows 20 times more, when there will be only 13 stitches; then knit 64 rows plain, always slipping the 1st stitch; this will make the bodice 25 inches round the waist, if required more or less, these 64 rows can be added to or reduced.

107th row—Increase a stitch thus—knit the 1st stitch; but before taking it off the left pin put the right pin into the back of the same stitch and knit it off—knit the rest plain.

108th row—Slip 1, knit the rest. Repeat the last 2 rows 20 times more, when there will be 34 stitches; then, commencing at the 1st row, repeat the direction once more.

297th row—(For the button-holes) Slip 1, knit 1 (make 1, knit 2 together, knit 4, 5 times), make 1, knit 2 together. Knit 5 rows plain and cast off. With the black wool doubled, and crochet-needle No. 1, work a row of single crochet on both sides of the selvedge of the band, working a stitch to each rib of the knitting.

THE RIGHT SIDE

With white wool and No. 10 pins cast on 27 stitches, and, as a guide to the making up, label the last stitch with the letter *a*. The work should be rather loose, so as to preserve the lightness of the wool.

1st row—Slip the 1st (make 1 and knit 2 together to the end), then cast on 6 stitches.

2nd row—Knit the 6 stitches cast on, and the rest of the 1st row all plain. Repeat these 2 rows 11 times more, when there will be 99 stitches. Mark the last stitch cast on, *b*.

25th row—Slip the 1st stitch, (make 1 and knit 2 together to the end).

26th row—Slip the 1st stitch, knit the rest plain. Repeat these 2 rows 8 times more. Then, at the longest side, cast off 8 stitches for the armhole, and mark it *c*. Work the 25th and 26th rows 14 times.

1st row—Make 1, knit 2 together, then knit 2 together again; repeat, and at the end knit 3. There will now be 69 stitches.

THE COLORED STRIPE—Join on the black wool, and use No. 19 pins for the next 8 rows. Knit 2 rows plain, with the colored wool knit 4 rows plain, and with the black knit 2 rows plain. Join on the white and work with No. 10 pins as before.

THE WHITE STRIPE, 1st row—Plain.

2nd row—Slip the 1st stitch, make 1 and knit 2 together to the end. Repeat these 2 rows 5 times more. Work a 2nd colored and white stripe, and a 3rd colored stripe. Join on the white and use No. 10 pins. Cast on 6 stitches for the back of the neck, work the 2 rows as the white stripe 19 times, then repeat the same 2 rows 8 times, but leaving 6 stitches at the end of the 2nd row each repeat. Cast off all the stitches.

The first and last rows of the white piece must now be sewed to the selvedge of the waistband at the side where the points are made; both pieces are to be kept on the wrong side, and in sewing it take the

Magenta stitches, leaving the black row in front. Sew the shortest side cast off to the top of the point at the back of the band, then sew the 1st stitch cast off to the 38th rib of the band. Take the end marked *a*, sew it close to this, and the end marked *b* to the centre point of the band. Gather the white and sew it to the band, placing more fulness at the points than under the arm; when finished, sew the sides together from the band to the armhole *c*.

THE LEFT SIDE—With the white wool and pins No. 10 cast on 27 stitches.

1st row—Plain. At the end cast on 6 stitches.

2nd row—Knit 2 together, * make 1, knit 2 together. Repeat from *, and at the end make 1, knit 1; mark this *a*. Repeat these 2 rows 11 times more, mark the last stitch cast on *b*. Then work the 2 rows 9 times, omitting the stitches cast on; and for the armhole cast off 8 stitches at the longest side, and repeat these 2 rows 14 times.

71st row—Plain.

72nd row—Make 1, knit 2 together twice, repeat, and at the end of the row knit 3.

Work the COLORED STRIPE as in the right side; and for

THE WHITE STRIPE, 1st row—Plain.

2nd row—Knit 2 together, * make 1, knit 2 together, Repeat from *, and at the end make 1, knit 1. Repeat these 2 rows 5 times more; then a 2nd colored and white stripe, and a third colored stripe. Join on the white, knit a plain row, cast on 6 stitches at the end of it and for

THE BACK, 1st row—Knit 2 together, * make one, knit 2 together. Repeat from *, and at the end make 1, knit 1.

2nd row—Plain. Repeat these 2 rows 18 times more; then work the same 2 rows 8 times, leaving 6 stitches at the end of the plain row each time. Cast off all the stitches, and sew it to the waistband, the same as the other side. The fronts are to be joined together to the 1st colored stripe.

THE POINTED TRIMMING

Commence with the black wool and No. 14 pins; cast on 421 stitches.

1st row—Black. Plain knitting; slip the 1st stitch of every row.

2nd row—Magenta. Slip 1, * make 1, knit 11, then knit 5 together, thus—slip 2, knit the next 3 stitches together, and turn the 2 slipped over them; knit 11, make 1, knit 1. Repeat from * to the end.

3rd row—Pearl knitting.

4th row—Slip 1, * make 1, knit 10, knit 5 together, knit 10, make 1, knit 1. Repeat

5th row—Pearl.

6th and 7th rows—Black. All plain.

8th row—Magenta. As the 4th row, knitting 9 stitches instead of 10 each time.

9th row—Pearl. Repeat the last 2 rows 3 times more, knitting one stitch less each time.

16th row—Slip 1, knit 6, * slip 1, knit 2 together, turn the slipped stitch over, knit 13. Repeat from *, and end with knit 7.

17th row—Pearl.

18th row—Slip 1, knit 5, * knit 3 together as before, knit 11. Repeat from *, and end with knit 6.

19th row—Pearl.

20th row—Black. Plain. Cast off, and sew it to the black row of the waistband. Each point must be sewed to the white bodice.

THE COLLAR—With black wool cast on 225 stitches. Work as the Pointed Trimming to the end of the 15th row, when, with black wool, knit a plain row, and cast off. Sew it to the neck of the bodice.

THE SLEEVES—With black wool cast on 197 stitches. Work as the collar, and sew it to the armhole.

SPANISH SLEEVE,

TO CORRESPOND WITH THE BODICE. No. 2.

Materials—1 skein each of Black, White, Blue or Magenta, Andalusian Wool; a pair of pins Nos. 19, 14, and 10.

With the black wool and No. 14 pins, cast on 169 stitches. Work as the Pointed Trimming in the previous direction to the end of the 20th row; knit the last two stitches of it together, when there will be 72 stitches on the pin; and for the

21st row—Black. All plain.

22nd row—Blue or Magenta; pins No. 19. Knit 1 and pearl 1 to the end. Work 15 rows more the same.

38th row—White; No. 10 pins. Make 1 and knit 3. Repeat, and knit the last 2 stitches together.

39th row—Plain.

40th row—Slip the 1st, then make 1, knit 2 together. Repeat to the end.

Work the last 2 rows 20 times more. Then with black wool and No. 19 pins knit 2 rows as the 22nd; with Magenta, knit 4 rows; and black, 2 rows the same. Cast off and sew the selvedges together. If required, the 2 rows of white can be repeated until it is sufficiently long to be attached to the armhole of the bodice.

GENTLEMAN'S RIFLE CRAVAT.

NETTING. No. 3.

Materials—1 skein each of Fawn and Scarlet, or Mauve and Black, Andalusian Wool; steel netting needle; a mesh No. 10, one No. 15, and a flat mesh one third of an inch wide.

Fill the needle with fawn or mauve wool, use No. 10 mesh, and commence by netting 140 stitches for the first row, and work 24 rows plain netting, increasing a stitch at the beginning of each row, by netting two stitches in the 1st stitch of each; then net 24 rows, netting 2 stitches together at the beginning of each row to decrease it.

THE BORDER—Run a string at one end of the work, about an inch from the slanting edge, so as to work on the selvedge.

1st row—Fill the needle with scarlet or black wool, and commence in the 10th stitch of the last row, counting from the end; then, with No. 10 mesh net these 10 stitches, then 12 stitches on the slanting side of the edge, 12 stitches on the other side, and 10 stitches on the 1st row; turn back.

2nd row—Flat mesh. Net 5 stitches in every other stitch of the 1st scarlet row.

3rd row—No. 15 mesh. Net 4 stitches, and, with the point of the needle, draw the next long stitch through the one missed of the 1st row, and net it. Repeat to the end and fasten off. Turn, and work the border to the other end the same. Join the 1st fawn row to the last to make it round, and with the scarlet wool embroider the Pattern at the end, as in the Section.

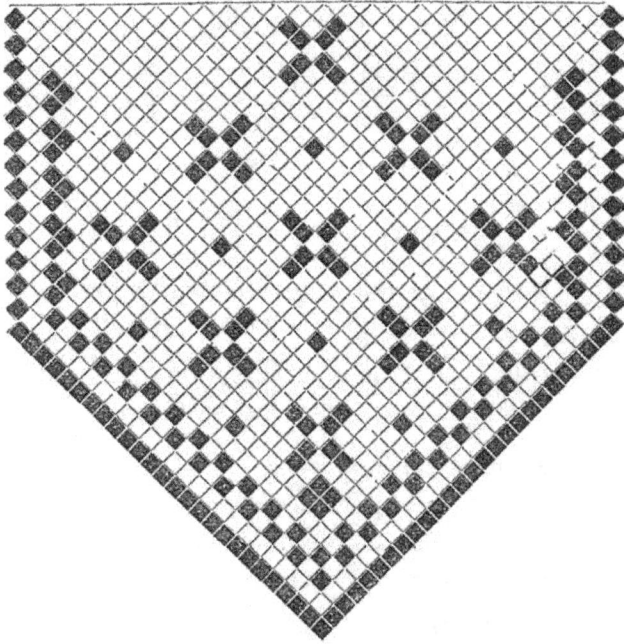

CRAVAT—SECTION OF EMBROIDERY PATTERN.

GENTLEMAN'S CUFF.

BRIOCHE KNITTING. No. 4.

Materials—1 skein each of White and Colored Andalusian Wool; 4 knitting needles, No. 16.

With the colored wool cast on 23 stitches on each of three needles—in all, 69 stitches.

1st round—Colored wool. Make 1, slip 1, knit 2 together. Repeat all round. Then tie on the white wool, turn back, so as to hold the work on the other side, leave the colored wool at the back on the right side, and with the white wool knit off the 3rd pin for the

2nd round—Make 1, slip 1, knit the 2 loops which cross together. Repeat all round. Bring the white wool in front, turn the work again, so as to hold it on the right side, keeping the white wool at the back, the colored being in the front. In commencing a round the wool should be kept tight. Repeat these 2 rounds about 50 times, and cast off.

CHILD'S SHOE.

TRICOT ECOSSAIS. No. 5.

Materials—1 skein each of Blue and White Andalusian wool; Tricot needle, the stem of which measures No. 14, Bell guage.

Commence at the back of the shoe with blue wool. Make a chain of 28 stitches.

1st double row—Raise the loops thus:—Keep the loop on the needle, miss the first chain stitch, * put the needle into the next stitch, and bring the wool through in a loop on the needle. Repeat from * until there are 28 loops on the needle; then, to "work back," take the wool on the needle, and bring it through the last 2 loops on it. Repeat, bringing the wool through 2 loops each time, until there are only 2 loops on the needle. Join on the white wool, still leaving the blue, and bring it through the 2 blue loops to finish the row. A double row is worked with the two colors alternately, throughout the shoe, and they need not be cut off; the end of every row is to be worked the same.

2nd row—White. Miss the edge stitch, and putting the needle into the perpendicular loop of the 1st row, bring the wool through; raise 9 loops more the same, and, to † increase a stitch, put the needle in the wool *between* the next 2 stitches and raise a loop; then raise a loop from the next stitch. Repeat from † 5 times more, than raise 12 loops as usual, when there will be 34 on the needle. Work back, as in the 1st row.

3rd row—Blue. Work a double row.

4th—White. Work a double row. Repeat these 2 double rows 9 times; making, in all, 22 rows.

23rd row—Blue. Make 8 chain, miss 1, raise 7 stitches from the 8 chain; then, on the 22nd row, raise 13 stitches as usual; increase a stitch, as before, then raise 8 stitches; increase a stitch, raise 13 stitches.

Take a piece of blue wool, make 8 chain, tie it to the last stitch of the 23rd row, and raise the 8 stitches of it; there will be 52 loops on the needle.

24th row—White. Work a double row of 52 stitches.

25th row—Blue. Raise all the stitches; but at the end take the last 2 stitches together to decrease a stitch. Work back until there are only 3 loops on the needle, then bring the white wool through all 3 to finish the row; this will decrease a stitch.

26th row—White. Miss the 2 loops close together, raise the rest of the loops as usual, and take the last 2 stitches together; work back to the last 3 loops, then bring the blue through them to finish.

Repeat as the last row, working the colors alternately, until there are only 20 stitches left, then with a rug-needle draw all these stitches together, and sew them firmly to form the toe. The stitches added at the 23rd row are for the instep, the shoe being joined up the front in single crochet, thus—work with the blue wool doubled; commence with a single stitch at the toe, place the slanting selvedges together, * put the needle into the right edge, then into the left edge, bring the wool through, and also through the loop on the needle. Repeat from * until the front is joined; fasten off.

For the back, double the 1st row and join the sides, drawing about 6 stitches together in the centre for the heel. Fold the blue wool in three, and with it work a row of single crochet along the top of the shoe, making a stitch to each double row; then, with the single wool, work a row of 1 chain, and 1 single in each stitch of the former row. Fasten off.

THE STRAP—Double the white wool, and with it make 66 chain, turn, miss 1, 4 single on the chain; then 3 chain, miss 3, and work single crochet along the remainder of the chain. Then with the blue wool, used single, work 1 chain and 1 single round both sides. Sew it to the back of the shoe, and a button to the strap opposite the button-holes.

A leather sole may be added, and the shoe lined with silk, if preferred, but it is complete without.

LADY'S NECKTIE,

IN POINTED NETTING. <u>No. 6.</u>

Materials—1 skein each of Magenta and Green Andalusian wool, or any two colours that contrast; 3 large steel netting needles and a mesh No. 10; a pair of tassels and ring.

A foundation of 241 stitches will be requisite.

1st row—Fill a needle with the Magenta wool, commence at the 1st stitch, and on the foundation net 60 stitches; then turn back, leaving the rest of the foundation, and net the 60 stitches; all the rows worked in Magenta are reckoned double rows.

2nd row—Net 55 stitches on the 1st row, and leaving 5 stitches of it, turn back and net the 55 stitches.

3rd row—Net 50 stitches, leaving 5 more, turn back and net the 50 stitches.

4th row—Net 45 stitches, turn back and net them.

5th row—Net 40 stitches, turn back and net them.

6th row—Net 35 stitches, turn back and net them. Leave the needle and this side of work.

Fill a second needle with Magenta, leave an end of wool and tie it in the 61st stitch of the foundation, counting from the other end of it, this will leave 120 stitches in the centre; net the 60 stitches, that is, to the end of the foundation, and repeat from the 2nd row to the end of the 6th row as before. There will now be half a point of Magenta at each end of the work; leave it, and fill a needle with green wool, and for

THE GREEN POINT, 1st row—Commence by joining the wool to the end of Magenta left at the beginning of the second half-point, then net the 120 stitches of the foundation, which will bring the wool to the 1st double row of Magenta, and, to join them together, pass the needle through the 1st loop of the Magenta, drawing it close to the work; and for the

2nd row—Net the 120 green stitches, then net the 5 Magenta stitches; pass the needle through the 1st loop of the 1st double row of the Magenta; turn back.

3rd row—Net the 125 green stitches, then 5 stitches on the Magenta at the other end; pass the needle through the loop to join it, and turn back. Work 8 rows more the same as the last, netting 5 stitches more each time; and, to diminish the point,

12th row—Net 165 stitches; this will leave 5 green; turn back.

13th row—Net 160 stitches, which will leave 5 green at the other end. Work 7 rows more as the last, netting 5 stitches less each time; the last row will be 125 stitches. Leave the needle and return to the 1st half-point of Magenta, and work for the

COMPLETE POINT, 1st row—Net 35 stitches, then 5 stitches on the 5 green, pass the needle through the 1st green loop to join it as before; turn back, and net the 40 stitches.

Net 4 double rows more the same, netting 5 stitches more each row; then net 5 double rows, leaving 5 Magenta stitches at the same side each row. Return to the other end, and repeat this point the same. Then work the green point, and repeat until there are four green points, which will be sufficient width. Then work only half the Magenta points at each side to correspond with the commencement. Join the 1st row to the last, draw up the ends, and sew on the tassels.

NETTED CUFF.

No. 7.

Materials—1 skein of Magenta, Blue, or Green, Andalusian Wool; 1 skein of Black Maltese silk; 2 steel netting needles; a flat ivory mesh, a quarter of an inch wide, and one half an inch wide; a steel mesh, No. 21.

The Cuff may either be commenced on a foundation or on a string of the black silk.

1st row—Fill a needle with the wool, and with the 1/4 inch mesh net 68 stitches. Leave the needle; fill the other needle with the black silk, and commence at the 1st stitch of the last row at the other end.

2nd row—Black, and No. 21 mesh. Net a plain row on the stitches of the last row; leave the black, both needles being now at the same side.

3rd row—Colored wool and 1/4 inch mesh. Net a plain row.

4th row—With the black at the other end, and 21 mesh, net a plain row. Repeat these 2 rows until there are 15 black and colored rows.

THE FRILL, 31st row—Colored wool and 1/2 inch mesh. Net 2 stitches in 1, then 1 plain in the next stitch; repeat, netting 2 stitches in each alternate stitch.

32nd row—Black, and No. 21 mesh. Net all the stitches of the last row. Fasten off.

Turn the string so as to work on the foundation row; net a row of black as before, then repeat the 31st and 32nd rows. Sew up the sides and double the cuff, so that the two frills are at the top.

BABY'S SOCK.

KNITTING. No. 8.

Materials—1 skein each of White and Magenta Andalusian wool; a small skein of Black Floss; 4 knitting needles, No. 18.

The chief part of this sock is worked on two needles, the others being used for the foot.

With white wool and 2 needles cast on 60 stitches for the leg.

1st row—Slip 1, knit 1, * pearl 2, and knit 2; repeat from *, ending with pearl 2. Work 27 rows more the same.

29th row—Make 1, knit 2 together; repeat. Then work 3 rows as the 1st.

33rd row—Make 1, knit 2 together; repeat.

34th and 35th rows—As the 1st.

36th row—Slip 1, pearl 49, this will leave 10 stitches; turn back, so as to work on the pearl stitches.

37th row—Slip 1, knit 39, this will leave 10 stitches at the other end.

38th row—Slip 1, pearl 39, put both the 10 stitches on 1 needle; they are for the instep, and will not be required until the heel is made. Repeat the last 2 rows twice more.

43rd row—Slip 1, knit 3, (pearl 1 and knit 7, 4 times), pearl 1, knit 3; these pearl stitches are to indicate where the color is to be worked when the sock is finished.

44th row—Slip 1, pearl 39. Work as the 37th and 38th rows 3 times more.

51st row—Slip 1 (knit 7 and pearl 1, 4 times), knit 7.

52nd row—Slip 1, pearl 39.

53rd row—Slip 1, knit 39.

54th row—As 52nd.

55th row—Slip 1, knit 14, knit 2 together (knit 2 and knit 2 together twice), knit 15.

56th row—Slip 1, knit 36.

57th row—Slip 1, knit 12, knit 2 together, knit 7, knit 2 together, knit 13.

58th row—Slip 1, knit 34.

59th row—Slip 1, knit 10, knit 2 together, knit 9, knit 2 together, knit 2, turn back, leaving 9 stitches.

60th row—Slip 1, knit 12, knit 2 together, knit 1, turn back, leaving 8 stitches.

61st row—Slip 1, knit 13, knit the last stitch and one of the 9 together; knit 16 rows more as the last, when there will be 15 stitches on the needle; and with the same needle raise 13 stitches from the selvedge formed by the side of the previous rows: then with another needle knit the 20 stitches left for the instep; take a 3rd needle and raise 13 stitches from the selvedge of the other side, and with the same needle knit 5 and knit 2 together on the 15 left stitches left for the heel; there will now be 60 stitches on the 3 needles.

THE FOOT, 1st round—Pearl the 1st stitch in the centre of the heel, knit the rest of the round plain. Work 7 rounds more the same.

9th round—Pearl 1, knit 16 (pearl 1 and knit 8, 3 times), pearl 1, knit 15. Work 9 rounds more as the 1st.

19th round—Pearl 1, knit 10; decrease by knitting 3 together thus— slip 1, knit 2 together, and turn the slipped stitch over; knit 7 (pearl 1 and knit 8 twice), pearl 1, knit 7, decrease as before, knit 10. Work 4 rounds as the 1st.

24th round—Pearl 1, knit 9, decrease, knit 31, decrease, knit 9. Work 4 rounds as the 1st.

29th round—Pearl 1, knit 8, decrease, knit 10, pearl 1, knit 8, pearl 1, knit 9, decrease, knit 8. Work 3 rounds as the 1st.

33rd round—Pearl 1, knit 7, decrease, knit 27, decrease, knit 7. Work 8 rounds as the 1st.

37th round—Pearl 1, knit 6, decrease, knit 3, pearl 1 (knit 8 and pearl 1 twice), knit 3 decrease, knit 6. Work 3 rounds as the 1st.

41st round—Pearl 1, knit 5, decrease, knit 23, decrease, knit 5. Work 3 rounds as the 1st.

45th round—Pearl 1, knit 4, decrease, knit 6, pearl 1, knit 8, pearl 1, knit 5, decrease, knit 4.

46th round—Pearl 1, knit the rest.

47th round—Pearl 1, knit 4, decrease, knit 17, decrease, knit 4.

48th—As 46th.

49th round—Pearl 1, knit 4, decrease, knit 13, decrease, knit 4.

50th—As 46th.

51st round—Pearl 1, knit 4, decrease, knit 4, pearl 1, knit 4, decrease, knit 4.

Then to join the toe, knit 5, turn the work on the wrong side, place the needles so as to double the stitches, and knit a stitch off each needle as one stitch 10 times. Fasten off. Sew up the leg. The sock should now be washed before the colored wool is worked.

THE TRIMMING, 1st round—Commence at the top and work with the colored wool and crochet needle No. 2, 5 chain, 1 plain in the centre of the knitted rib; repeat 14 times.

2nd round—Turn back so as to work the contrary way, keep the last round down in the front and work on the foundation round of the knitting as before; 5 chain and 1 plain in the centre of the pearled rib. Repeat all round.

3rd round—White. 4 chain, 1 plain in the next loop of chain of the 2nd round, 6 chain; 1 plain in the same loop of chain as before. Repeat all round.

4th round—Colored. 1 plain in the 4 chain of the last round, * 5 chain, 1 plain in the 6 chain, 7 chain, 1 plain in the same 6 chain, then 5 chain, 1 plain in the 4 chain. Repeat from *, and fasten off.

Turn this frill down over the sock, then with a rug needle and black floss work a chain stitch at every other point of the trimming, to attach it to the 20th row of the sock.

The Spots are now to be embroidered at every pearled stitch of the sock, thus—with black floss commence at the centre of the toe, work a chain stitch over the 1 pearl, taking it across 2 stitches of the knitting in width, and 3 rows in depth. Repeat at each pearl stitch of the front and sides, slipping the needle along on the wrong side; then with the colored wool work a chain stitch at each of the black stitches, commencing one stitch lower, and working it in the centre of the black.

The cord is made by working a chain with the colored wool doubled, and it is to be run in both open rows, and finished with tassels.

KNITTED SOCK.

FOR A CHILD OF ABOUT THREE YEARS OF AGE. No. 9.

Materials—1 skein each of Black and Mauve Andalusian Wool; 5 knitting needles, No. 19.

This Sock can be made in a plain colour if preferred, it will measure 7 inches round the top of the leg, 7 inches in depth, and the foot six inches long; it can be made a size larger or smaller by varying the needles.

Commence at the top of the leg, and with the mauve wool cast on 16 stitches on each of four needles, using the 5th to make it round, in all, 64 stitches, these should be cast on with 2 needles that it may be loose.

1st round—Pearl 2 and knit 2 alternately all round. Work 3 rounds more the same. Leave the mauve wool, and with the black work 2 more rounds as before. Repeat these 6 rounds 4 times more, in all, 30 rounds. When the wools are changed, they should be twisted together.

31st round—Mauve. Pearl the 1st stitch, knit the rest plain. Work 3 rounds more the same. Then with black work 2 rounds more the same. Repeat these 6 rounds twice more.

49th round—Mauve. Pearl 1, knit 2 together, knit the rest, knitting the last 2 stitches together. Then work 3 mauve rounds as the 31st; then black, 2 rounds; mauve, 4 rounds; and black, 2 rounds the same.

61st round—As the 49th. Then work 3 rounds as the 31st, and 2 black the same. Work as the 31st and 5 following rounds 4 times more. There will now be 15 mauve and black stripes from the commencement. Then, with the needle on which the last stitches were worked, take the first 15 stitches off the 1st needle without knitting them; turn on the wrong side, so as to work on the stitches taken off; commence with the mauve wool, and for

THE HEEL, 1st row—Slip 1, pearl 13, knit 1; this is the stitch pearled in the previous rounds, pearl 14, turn back, leaving 31 stitches for the instep.

2nd row—Slip 1, knit 13, pearl 1, knit 14, turn back.

3rd row—As the 1st.

4th row—As the 2nd.

5th row—Black. As the 1st.

6th row—As the 2nd.

Repeat these 6 rows 4 times more.

31st row—Slip 1, pearl 16, pearl 2 together, pearl 10.

32nd row—Slip 1, knit 14, knit 2 together, taking the back of the stitches, knit 1, turn back, leaving 10 stitches.

33rd row—Slip 1, pearl 5, pearl 2 together, pearl 1, turn back.

34th row—Slip 1, knit 6, knit 2 together as before, knit 1, turn back.

35th row—Black, passing it across on the wrong side, pearl 8, pearl 2 together, pearl 1.

36th row—Slip 1, knit 8, knit 2 together, knit 1.

37th row—Mauve. Pearl 10, pearl 2 together, pearl 1.

38th row—Slip 1, knit 10, knit 2 together, knit 1.

39th row—Slip 1, pearl 11, pearl 2 together, pearl 1.

40th row—Slip 1, knit 12, knit 2 together, knit 1.

41st row—Black. Pearl 14, pearl 2 together, pearl 1.

42nd row—Slip 1, knit 14, knit 2 together, knit 1. Knot the wools together.

THE FOOT, 1st round—Mauve. Commence at the 31 stitches left for the instep, knit them on to one needle, and with another needle raise 17 stitches from the selvedge of the rows knitted for the back of the heel. Take another needle, knit the 17 black stitches; take another needle, raise 17 stitches from the other selvedge, then knit 1 stitch off the 1st needle, there will be in all 82 stitches on the 4 needles.

2nd round—Pearl 1, knit 27, pearl 1, slip 1, knit 1, and turn the slipped stitch over it, knit 49, then knit the last 2 stitches together.

3rd round—All plain.

4th round—Pearl 1, knit 27, pearl 1, slip 1, knit 1, turn over, knit 47, knit the last 2 together.

5th round—Black. All plain.

6th row—Black. As the 4th. Knitting 45 stitches instead of 47.

7th round—Mauve. All plain. Then, commencing at the 2nd round, repeat the last 6 rounds twice more, working 2 stitches less between the decreased stitches each time.

20th round—Mauve. Pearl 1, knit 27, pearl 1, knit the rest.

21st round—All plain.

22nd round—As the 20th.

Then work 2 rounds plain of black and 4 of mauve alternately 8 times, pearling the 1st and 29th stitch of every other round. Then 2 rounds the same of black and fasten it off, the sock being finished with mauve.

THE TOE, 1st round—Knit 1 (knit 2 together, and knit 5, 9 times), then 5 rounds plain, pearling the 2 stitches in the alternate rounds as before.

7th round—Knit 1 (knit 2 together, and knit 4, 9 times); then 3 rounds plain as before.

11th round—Knit 1 (knit 2 together, and knit 3, 9 times); then 3 rounds plain as before.

15th round—Knit 1 (knit 2 together, and knit 2, 9 times); then 1 round plain as before.

17th round—Knit 1 (knit 2 together, and knit 1, 9 times). Draw the remaining stitches together and fasten off.

OPERA HOOD.

PLAIN KNITTING. No. 10.

Materials—1/2 oz. of Black and 1-1/2 ozs. each of White and Colored Andalusian wool; 1 reel of Gold Check; a pair of Knitting Pins No. 7; and for the Trimming, Crochet Needle No. 1.

THE FRONT

THE WHITE STRIPE.—With white wool, cast on very loosely with 2 pins, 90 stitches. Work 10 rows plain knitting, always slipping the 1st stitch of each row; then for

THE COLORED STRIPE—Black wool. Knit two rows plain as before.

Colored wool. 4 rows.

Gold check. 4 rows.

Colored wool. 4 rows.

Black wool. 2 rows.

THE WHITE STRIPE—Knit 14 rows plain. Repeat the colored stripe and 12 rows of white; then knit 2 rows of white, casting off very loosely 14 stitches at the beginning of each row. These ends are for the Lappets, and 62 stitches will be left in the centre; on these 62 stitches repeat the colored stripe and 10 rows of white. Cast off loosely, so that the work may be stretched lengthways and measure about one yard, including the lappets, which are now to be fringed as follows:

THE FRINGE—Cut the white wool in lengths of 6 inches, take 3 pieces, and put the crochet needle into a stitch of the selvedge of a white stripe, fold the wools on the point of the needle, bring them through the stitch in a loop, then bring the ends of wool through the loop and draw them tight. Repeat along the selvedge, looping in the same colors as the stripes. Fringe the opposite lappet the same. Then, with a rug-needle and wool commence at the 14th stitch of the foundation row, run it across the stripes, so as to draw them all together, and sew it firm; to this will be attached the strings and a rosette. Draw the other end the same; then, commencing at the centre stitch of the foundation draw the stripes together for the middle of the head, where the large rosette is placed.

THE BACK

WHITE STRIPE—With white wool, cast on tightly with 1 pin, 20 stitches.

1st row—Knit the 1st stitch; but before taking it off the left pin put the right pin into the back of the same stitch, and knit it off—this will increase a stitch. Repeat to the end, when there will be 40 stitches. Knit 9 rows plain as before.

Repeat the colored stripe and 14 rows of white as for the front, until there are 6 white stripes and 5 colored; in the last repeat, work only 9 white rows, and for the last row knit every 2 stitches together, and cast off tightly.

Fringe one selvedge of this piece in the same manner as the lappets.

THE ROSETTES—With the crochet needle and black wool work 5 chain, and make it round.

1st round—Work 10 plain crochet stitches in the round loop.

2nd round—Join on the gold check, work 4 chain and 1 plain on the lower edge of the black stitches, leaving the upper edge at the back. Repeat 9 times more.

3rd round—Colored wool. 7 chain, 1 plain on the upper edge of the black row left at the back of the last. Repeat all round.

4th round—Black wool. 10 chain and 1 plain in the back of the same black stitch in which the colored one was worked. Repeat all round and fasten off. Sew this rosette to the centre row of the 2nd White Stripe of the Back, about 12 stitches from the edge which is fringed, then draw up the 12 stitches under the rosette, so that it touches the edge and forms a scallop. Work 3 rosettes more the same, attaching them to the 3 following white stripes. 5 more rosettes will be required. Sew one to each side where the front is drawn together at the lappets.

LARGE ROSETTE—Commence with the colored wool; work 20 chain, make it round, and work 10 chain and 1 plain 16 times in the round loop. Join on the black wool, and work 12 chain and 1 plain 16 times, putting the needle in the same foundation chain as before, but at the back of the colored round; then, with the gold check, commence in a loop of the black round, work 5 chain and 1 plain in each black loop. Repeat, and fasten off. Take a small rosette and sew it into the centre of the large one; then attach it to the centre of the front, where the stitches were drawn together.

The back and front are to be joined together by sewing the selvedge of the side not fringed to the foundation row of the front, thus—keep the back piece on the right side of the work, and the front on the wrong side, as it is to turn over to form a roll round the face, attach the corners of the back piece under the rosettes at the top of the lappets. Draw together the selvedge of the 3 colored stripes in the middle of the back piece, and sew it under the large rosette; then sew the rest of the selvedge to the 1st row of the front, and turn it over on the right side; on each side attach a rosette to the 2nd white stripe of the back near the front.

THE CORD is made by folding the wools 6 times; take a length of about 1-1/2 yards of black, colored, and gold, plait them together; two lengths will be required. Leave 16 inches for the strings, and tack the rest to the back, as in the engraving. A tassel is to be made at each end of the cord.

BABY'S GAUNTLET MUFFATEE.

KNITTING. No. 11.

Materials—1 skein each of Black and Colored Andalusian Wool; a pair of Knitting Pins No. 18, and a pair No. 13.

THE GAUNTLET—With colored wool and pins No. 13 cast on 57 stitches.

1st row—Pearl knitting. At the beginning of every row slip the 1st stitch.

2nd row—Plain knitting.

3rd row—Black wool. Pearl.

4th row—Slip the 1st stitch; then make 1 and knit 2 together to the end.

5th row—Colored wool. Pearl.

6th row—Plain.

7th row—Pearl.

Now use the black wool and small pins for the next 4 rows.

8th and 9th rows—Plain.

10th row—Pearl.

11th row—Plain.

Use the colored wool and the large pins.

12th row—Plain.

13th row—As the 4th.

Repeat the last 2 rows 8 times more.

Then use the small pins and black wool.

30th row—Slip the 1st, then knit 3 plain and knit 2 together to the end. There will now be only 46 stitches.

31st row—Plain.

32nd row—Pearl.

33rd row—Plain.

Use the large pins and colored wool.

34th row—Plain.

35th row—As the 4th.

Repeat the last 2 rows 6 times more.

Use the small pins and black wool.

48th and 49th rows—Plain.

50th row—Pearl.

51st row—Plain.

This finishes the Gauntlet; and for

THE HAND—Use colored wool, still working with the small pins. Knit 32 rows plain.

33rd row—Slip 1, knit 30, and, to form the thumb, turn back, leaving 15 stitches; and on the 31 stitches slip 1, knit 15; raise a stitch between the stitches, and turn back, leaving 15 stitches at the other end; and on the 17 stitches, slip 1, knit 16, raise a stitch; and on these 18 stitches, knit 12 rows plain; then slip 1 (knit 2 together, and knit 2, 4 times), knit 1, turn back, and knit a plain row; then slip 1, knit 2 together, knit 3, knit 2 together, knit 4, knit 2 together, turn back and knit a plain row; then knit 2 together 4 times, and with a rug needle draw up the remaining stitches and sew them firm. Sew the two selvedges together to make it round.

To finish the Hand, hold the work on the right side, so that the thumb is in front. Join on the wool at the left side of the thumb, and with the right pin knit the 15 stitches off the left pin.

34th row—Slip 1, knit 14, raise 2 stitches at the thumb, knit the other 15 stitches, then 20 rows plain.

55th row—Slip 1, knit 2 together, knit 9, knit 2 together, knit 3, knit 2 together, knit 9, knit 2 together, knit 2.

56th row—Plain.

Repeat the last 2 rows 4 times more, knitting 2 stitches less at the 9 plain each time. Draw up the remaining stitches and sew the selvedges together. Fold the 1st row, and sew it over to the 7th row, so that the 4th row may form the edge.

FOOT-MUFF.

KNITTING. No. 12.

Materials—3 skeins each of Magenta and Black 12-ply Fleecy, or any two colours that contrast; a pair of large Knitting Pins 1-1/2 inches in circumference. For the Lining, 1/2lb of White or Grey Fleecy, and a pair of Knitting Pins No. 1.

THE FRONT

With the black wool and large pins cast on 36 stitches, leave it and tie on the other color.

1st row—Magenta. Bring the wool in front of the pin, slip a stitch, pass the wool to the back, knit the next stitch; repeat to the end.

2nd row—Keep the wool at the back, slip the Magenta stitch, bring the wool in front, pearl the black stitch, pass the wool to the back, and repeat to the end.

3rd row—Black. Bring the wool in front, slip 1, pass the wool to the back, knit 1; repeat.

4th row—Slip the black stitch, bring the wool in front, pearl the Magenta stitch, pass the wool to the back, and repeat.

Work these 4 rows 13 times more, when it should measure about 14 inches wide and 10 inches deep.

To shape the top, with Magenta work as the 1st row for 10 stitches, turn back, leaving the rest, and on these 10 stitches work as the 2nd row, turn back; then with black work as the 3rd row for 8 stitches, knit 2 together, turn back; knit 1, then 8 stitches as the 4th row, turn back; work 6 stitches as the 1st row, knit 3 together, turn back; knit 1, then 6 stitches as the 2nd row, turn back; work 4 stitches as the 3rd row, knit 3 together, turn back; pearl 3 together, pearl 2, cast off the 3 stitches, and fasten the wools.

Commence at the stitches left, and with Magenta knit 2 together, then work as the 1st row for 12 stitches, knit 2 together, turn back; knit 1, work as the 2nd row for 12 stitches, knit 1, turn back. Join on the black, knit 3 together, then 8 stitches as the 3rd row, knit 3 together, turn back; knit 1, then 6 stitches as the 4th row, pearl 3 together, turn back; knit 1, then 6 stitches as the 1st row, knit 1, turn back; pearl 3 together, then 4 stitches as the 2nd row, knit 1, cast off.

Commence with Magenta at the stitches left, and knit as the 1st row for the 10 stitches, turn back; work as the 2nd row for 10 stitches, turn back. Join on the black, knit 2 together, then 8 stitches as the 3rd row, turn back; work 8 stitches as the 4th row, knit 1, turn back. Then with Magenta, knit 3 together, then 6 stitches as the 1st row, turn back; knit 6 stitches as the 2nd row, knit 1, turn back; with black, knit 3 together, then 4 stitches as the 3rd row, turn back; pearl 2, pearl 3 together, cast off.

THE SIDES AND BACK

With black wool cast on 80 stitches, and work the first 4 rows the same as for the front. Repeat these 4 rows again. Then work the same 4 rows 4 times more, leaving 4 stitches unworked at the end of each row to slant the sides. Put all the stitches on one pin, and cast them off.

THE LINING

With the white wool and No. 1 pins cast on 39 stitches. As a guide to the making up, the first of these stitches should be labeled A, and the last B.

1st row—Make 1, slip 1, knit 2 together; repeat to the end. Then cast on 3 stitches.

Work 19 rows more the same, casting on 3 stitches at the end of each. Then 2 rows without casting on. There will now be 33 ribs on the pin.

23rd row—Cast off 30 stitches or 10 ribs, work the rest of the row as before.

24th row—Cast off 10 ribs at the other end; this will leave 13 ribs in the centre; the stitches cast off are for the sides of the lining. On these 13 ribs now work 120 rows.

To shape the top, knit 4 ribs, turn back, and knit these 4 ribs backwards and forwards for 5 rows more; then knit 8 ribs, turn back and knit them; then 2 ribs, turn back and knit them; then 1 rib, turn back and knit it; cast off these 12 stitches, and label the first one B, then on the stitches left knit 5 ribs, turn back, and on the 5 ribs knit 5 rows. Then 4 rows, leaving a rib at the end of each, turn back, knit 3 ribs, then cast off these 5 ribs, and on the 4 ribs knit 7 rows; then 3 double rows, leaving a rib at the end of each. Cast off, label it A. The Lining is folded at about the centre of the 120 straight rows; the foundation row being for the top of the back; attach A to A and B to B, then sew the stitches cast off for the sides to one-half of the selvedge of the straight rows, and the stitches cast on to the other half.

The work, when finished, should be mounted on a frame of millboard, with a cord to correspond at the seams, and a rouleau of shaded grey wool round the opening.

CANADIAN RAILWAY WRAPPER,

COUVRE PIED, ETC.

KNITTING. No. 13.

Materials—6 ounces each of Black, Magenta, Green, Mauve, and Amber 12-ply Fleecy; a pair of short Knitting Pins, No. 1; and for the Joining, Tricot Needle, No. 5.

MAGENTA STRIPE—Cast on 11 stitches.

1st row—Make 1, knit 4, slip 1, knit 2 together, turn the slipped stitch over the two knitted together, knit 4.

2nd row—Keep the wool in front of the pin and turn it round it, so as to make a stitch, then pearl 10 stitches.

Repeat these 2 rows until 1-1/4 yards or the required length is made. Then, to form the point to correspond with the commencement, make 1, knit 2 together, knit 2, knit 3 together as usual, knit 2, knit 2 together; turn back, make 1, pearl 8; turn back, make 1, knit 2 together, knit 1, knit 3 together, knit 1, knit 2 together; turn back, make 1, pearl 2 together, pearl 2, pearl 2 together; turn back, knit 1, knit 3 together, knit 1; turn back, pearl 3 together, and fasten off.

Work 2 more Magenta stripes, then 2 green, and 2 mauve. The Magenta are for the centre and two ends, the latter being omitted in the engraving for want of space. If required still wider add a green stripe at each end.

BLACK STRIPE—Cast on 3 stitches.

1st row—Make 1, knit 2 together, knit 1. Repeat until the same length is made as the straight side of the colored stripes.

TO JOIN THE STRIPES—Amber wool and crochet needle. Make a chain stitch, take one of the Magenta stripes and work a single stitch on the 1st stitch of it, keep the loop on the needle. Take a black stripe, put the needle into the 1st loop at the side of it, bring the amber through, and also through the loop on the needle. Put the needle into the next loop at the side of the colored stripe, taking two folds of the wool to make it firm, bring the amber wool through, and also through the loop on the needle; continue working a single stitch alternately on each stripe until they are joined. The other stripes are joined in the same manner; when finished, with amber wool work a row of 1 chain and 1 single up one side of the last stripe, then along the top work a single row, and down the other side 1 chain and 1 single, then a single row along the other end.

THE FRINGE—Cut the wool in lengths of 8 inches, and loop it into the single row, putting in a black loop and a loop the same color as the stripe alternately along each point.

LADY'S STOCKING.

KNITTING.

Materials—White, Brown, Violet, or Scarlet Andalusian Wool; 5 knitting needles, No. 20.

Commence at the top of the leg, cast on 31 stitches on each of 4 needles, in all 124 stitches. Keep the 5th needle to make it round.

1st round—Knit 2 and pearl 2; repeat all round. Work 41 rounds more the same.

43rd round—Pearl the first stitch, knit the rest plain.

Work 140 rounds plain, but pearling the 1st stitch of every alternate round, which is to be continued to the end of the heel to form the seam; then to decrease the leg,

184th round—Knit 1, knit 2 together, knit the rest plain to the last 2 stitches, then knit 1, slip 1, turn the slipped stitch over the knitted one, which will make the decrease stitches correspond with the other side of the seam.

Knit 4 rounds plain, still pearling the seam stitch. Repeat the last 5 rounds 18 times more, when it will be reduced to 86 stitches.

Knit 82 rounds plain as before.

Then to shape the Heel, pearl 1, knit 22, turn back so as to work on the last stitches; and for the

1st row—Slip 1, pearl 44, turn back.

2nd row—Slip 1, knit 21, pearl the seam, knit 22, turn back; these 45 stitches should all be on one needle, and the remaining 41 stitches are to be kept on two of the needles until required for the front. Repeat these 2 rows 29 times more.

61st row   Slip 1, pearl the rest.

62nd row—Slip 1, knit 19, knit 2 together, pearl 1, slip 1, knit 1, turn over, knit 20. Repeat the last 2 rows 3 times more, working one stitch less each time before decreasing; then slip 1, pearl 18. Place the two needles together, so as to double the work, and with the 3rd needle slip 1, then knit a stitch off each pin together, turn the slipped stitch over, knit a stitch off each pin together again, turn the 1st stitch over, and repeat until these stitches are cast off.

THE INSTEP—Commence at the last stitch of the 41 left on the needle, and with the 3rd needle raise 36 stitches from the selvedge of the rows at the right side of the heel. Take another needle and raise 36 stitches from the left side of the selvedge; and for the

- 33 -

1st round—Knit the 41 stitches on the two needles, then on the stitches which were raised pearl 1, knit 70, pearl 1.

2nd round—All plain.

3rd round—Knit 41, pearl 1, slip 1, knit 1, turn over, knit 66, knit 2 together, pearl 1.

Repeat the last 2 rounds 13 times more, knitting 2 stitches less at the 66 stitches each time. Then work 63 rounds plain, pearling the 2 seam stitches every alternate round.

93rd round—Knit 2 together, knit 37, slip 1, knit 1, turn over, pearl 1, knit 2 together, knit 38, slip 1, knit 1, turn over, pearl 1.

94th round—All plain. Repeat these 2 rounds 12 times more, knitting 2 stitches less between each of the decreases; then double the remaining stitches and cast them off the same as at the heel.

IN THE PRESS,

PRICE ONE SHILLING

A new style of Work for

DOYLEYS, ANTIMACASSARS,

&c., &c., &c.

UNDER THE PATRONAGE OF

ROYALTY
AND
The Aristocracy of Europe,
AND
UNIVERSALLY IN HIGH REPUTE.

ROWLANDS' MACASSAR OIL

Is a delightfully Fragrant and Transparent Preparation for the Hair, and as an *invigorator and beautifier*, beyond all precedent. It bestows a permanent gloss, with a silky softness, and a strong tendency to curl, and is THE ONLY KNOWN SPECIFIC capable of effectually sustaining the hair in decorative attractiveness during the exercise of dancing, or the relaxing effects of crowded rooms. Price 3*s*. 6*d*. and 7*s*.; Family Bottles (equal to four small), 10*s*. 6*d*.; and double that size, 21*s*. per bottle.

ROWLANDS' KALYDOR,

FOR THE SKIN AND COMPLEXION,

A Balmy, Odoriferous Creamy Liquid, as equally celebrated for safety in application as unequalled for its rare and inestimable qualities. The radiant bloom it imparts to the cheek, the softness and delicacy which it induces of the hands and arms, its capability of soothing irritation, and removing cutaneous defects, discolorations, and all unsightly appearances, render it indispensable to every toilet. Price 4*s*. 6*d*. and 8*s*. 6*d*. per Bottle.

ROWLANDS' ODONTO,

OR PEARL DENTIFRICE,

a White Powder, compounded of the *choicest* and most *recherché* ingredients of the Oriental Herbal, and of inestimable value in preserving and imparting a Pearl-like Whiteness to the Teeth, eradicating Tartar and spots of incipient Decay, strengthening the Gums, and in giving fragrance to the Breath. Price 2*s.* 9*d.* per Box.

Sold by A. ROWLAND & SONS, 20, Hatton Garden, London,

And by Chemists and Perfumers.

▯ *Ask for* "ROWLANDS'" *Articles, and beware of Spurious Imitations!*

CPSIA information can be obtained
at www.ICGtesting.com
Printed in the USA
LVHW052355021121
702257LV00007B/897

9 789355 346841